Among Angels

Among Angels

by Jane Seymour

Guideposts
New York, New York

Among Angels

ISBN-13: 978-0-8249-4850-4

Published by Guideposts
16 East 34th Street
New York, NY 10016
www.guideposts.com

Distributed by Ideals Publications, a division of Guideposts
2630 Elm Hill Pike, Suite 100
Nashville, TN 37214

Guideposts and Ideals are registered trademarks of Guideposts.

Library of Congress Cataloging-in-Publication Data

Seymour, Jane, 1951-
  Among angels / by Jane Seymour.
      p. cm.
  ISBN 978-0-8249-4850-4
  1. Angels--Christianity--Miscellanea. I. Title.
  BT966.3.S48 2010
  235'.3--dc22
                          2010018197

Cover design by Georgia Morrissey
Cover and interior art by Jane Seymour
Back cover photograph by CharlesWilliamBush.com
Interior design and typesetting by Maria Taffera Lewis

10 9 8 7 6 5 4 3 2 1

To my family, friends and fans
        who support, encourage and inspire me
to recognize the angels among us.

A very special thanks to my sister Annie
        for all of her help, and Sally for her support.

In memory of our parents and special angels
        John and Mieke, Stacy and Mary,
as well as Chris and Dana Reeve and
        Johnny and June Cash.

Contents

OPEN YOUR HEART TO ANGELS

After I wrote *Open Hearts*, I received letters from people around the world with stories of how living with an open heart had changed their lives. When describing the great love—between family members, friends, and even strangers—one word was used over and over again: *angel*.

I don't think it's a coincidence that acts of love and visions of angels go hand in hand.

Angels have appeared universally throughout history: in folklore, in art and in every major religion. Most people have their own angel stories, whether they call them such or not. Be it a chance meeting, perfect timing, a bit of luck, a close call or an all-out miracle, we've all been touched by something extraordinary.

As I thought about my own encounters with angels and began to paint, draw and design jewelry out of that inspiration, I saw familiar faces. In many instances the angels in my life were people I knew: my mother, my father, my friends, my dear fans. I believe that angels walk among us, inspire us and in many cases, *are* us.

I hope this collection of true stories, beautiful prose and my own artwork will inspire you, remind you to keep a look out for angels among us and help ignite the angel within.

Jane Seymour

"If you seek an angel
with an open heart...
You shall always find one."

{ Author Unknown }

Jane Seymour

A World of Angels

WRITTEN ON OUR HEARTS

Angels are prominent figures

in almost every religion and culture.

Spirits called to help humanity appear

not just in Christianity and Judaism,

but also in Islam, Hinduism and the worship systems

in China, Japan and Africa.

I don't think it's a coincidence that the same idea was written

onto human hearts around the world.

DO YOU?

GROW! GROW!

*W*e all have angels whispering in our ears to reach up, to reach out, to reach our greatest potential. All we have to do is listen.

Every blade of grass has its angel
that bends over it and whispers,

"Grow, grow."

{ The Talmud }

He shall give his ANGELS charge over thee,

to keep THEE:

And in their hands they shall bear thee up,

Lest at any time thou dash thy foot against a stone.

{ *Luke 4:10-11* }

SHELTERING ANGELS

*H*ow wonderful life is when we choose to fill it
with laughter and friendship.
I find my dearest friends shelter me just like angels.

"May God grant you always:
A sunbeam to warm you,
A moonbeam to charm you,
A sheltering angel so nothing can harm you.
Laughter to cheer you. Faithful friends near you.
And whenever you pray, heaven to hear you."

{ *Irish Blessing* }

SUNSHINE IN THE SHADOWS

Like angels, we have the power to spread light and love. Simple things, like a smile to a stranger, can cast sunshine on even the darkest days.

"I will not wish thee riches, nor the glow

of greatness, but that wherever thou go

some weary heart shall gladden at thy smile,

or shadowed life know sunshine for a while.

And so thy path shall be a track of light,

like angels' footsteps passing through the night."

{ Words on a Church Wall in Upwaltham, England }

{ 19 }

A LIFETIME OF HOPE

Angela Brunette was told by doctors to prepare herself and her seven-year-old daughter Christina for the inevitable. The little girl had an inoperable tumor on her spine, and she had a very small chance of survival.

One morning, Christina's five-year-old sister, who shared a room with Christina, woke up and assured her mom that Christina would be "all better." She explained that she had seen an enormous angel almost as tall as the ceiling standing at the foot of Christina's bed. Soon after, Angela had two dreams herself of a hand coming from the ceiling and healing Christina while an angel stood by. These visions of angels made them think of the scriptures in the Bible where God assures us that He

sends his angels to watch over us. Angela remarked that
seeing these visions of angels watching over her daughter
reminded her of how great God's love is for her child and
how she can trust Him to take care of her no matter
the outcome.

At Christina's next hospital visit, her doctors were
shocked to discover that her tumor had completely
disappeared.

The Brunette family was so thankful to God, they
decided to spend the rest of their lives sharing their
hope and joy. They created a charity called Basket of
Hope that delivers inspiration to seriously ill children
and their families in over sixteen hospitals around the
country, reminding them that God loves them. Thousands
of kids have been touched by love...all because of one little girl,
her mom, and their angel, a messenger of hope from the Lord.

MY GUARDIAN DEAR

"Angel of God, my guardian dear
to whom God's love commits me here;
Ever this day be at my side,
to light and guard, to rule and guide."

{ Old English Prayer }

BLESSED SPECTATORS

*H*ow comforting it is to know that we are not alone! Even when we cannot see
them, we carry with us the love of family, friends and the angels above.

We not only live among men, but there are airy hosts,

Blessed spectators, sympathetic lookers-on,
that see and know

And appreciate our thoughts and feelings and acts.

{ *Henry Ward Beecher* }

HEAVEN IS VISIBLE

As much of heaven
is visible
as we have eyes to see.

{ William Winter }

Finding Your Angel

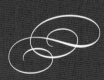

ANGELS ALL AROUND US

I believe that angels are all around us all the time.

We just don't always see them.

Take the time to really see the angels in your life.

SEEK THEM. FIND THEM.

Open your hearts to them,

for they are waiting for you with

OPEN *hearts* and OPEN *arms.*

It's AMAZING what can truly happen,

how your life can be so GRAND;

when you GIVE UP trying on your own,

and let an ANGEL hold your hand.

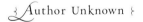 Author Unknown ∤

NOT A CHANCE ENCOUNTER

*H*ow often have we found ourselves in a situation that was frightening
when someone or something suddenly appeared and helped us?
Are these not encounters with angels?

Make yourself familiar with the angels,
and behold them frequently in spirit;
for without being seen, they are present
with you.

{ *St.* Francis de *S*ales }

THE POWER OF VISION

An angel can illuminate
the thought and mind of man
by strengthening
the power of vision.

{ *St.* Thomas Aquinas }

LIFESAVER

My husband James is still thankful—as am I!—that a mysterious stranger appeared and saved his life:

The same day I passed my open-water scuba test, my instructor and I went spearfishing. When he swam off to find a fish, I surfaced because my air tank was about to go on reserve. We had been taught never to dive alone and to always be near our dive partner, so I made it clear that I would wait for him on the surface. I waited and waited, but my instructor never returned. I thought maybe he was in trouble, so I turned down to look for him under the kelp pod. My weight belt, tank and knife got tangled in the thick kelp when I got caught in a strong current.

As the undertow pulled me up and down, I found myself struggling to keep my head above water in order to breathe. My tank had run completely out of air. When I realized I was drowning, I screamed "Help!" for the first time in my life before I was pulled under into the thick kelp. I was taking in lots of water as I kicked with all my might to stay above the ocean's surface. I was getting weaker by the second with each surge of the sea. I remember seeing our dive boat in the distance, and someone jumping into the water. Although logic would have said to go under the water to save someone drowning, he was swimming on top of the sea over the kelp pads. Having taken on so much saltwater that my lungs were filled, I passed out.

I then saw myself from above, lying on the deck of the boat, someone pounding on my chest to pump the water out of my lungs. It turns out the lifeguard on my boat could not swim. The man who jumped in and saved me was on the boat watching as his own son took the same open-water scuba test that I had. Amazingly, he had just passed an open-water *scuba rescue course* the very night before. Had he not been there and known the only way to get through the kelp was to swim over it, I would not be here today. He was my angel.

{ James Reach }

Everything Is A Miracle

There are only two ways

to live your life.

One is as though

NOTHING IS A MIRACLE.

The other is as though

EVERYTHING IS A MIRACLE.

⦃ Albert Einstein ⦄

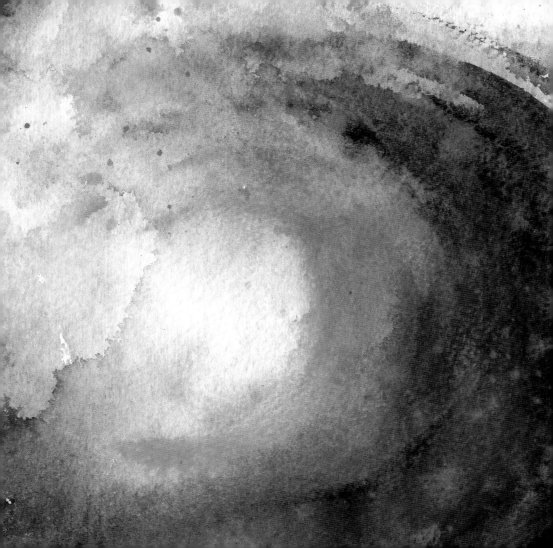

BLESSINGS WITHOUT NUMBER

Hush! My dear, lie still and slumber.

Holy Angels guard thy bed!

Heavenly blessings without number

Gently falling on thy head.

{ Isaac Watts }

E N T E R T A I N I N G   A N G E L S

Since childhood we've heard The Golden Rule: Treat others as you wish to be treated. The problem is we often neglect to treat ourselves well. What if, instead, we treated others as if they were angels?

Be not forgetful to entertain strangers, for
Thereby some have entertained angels
unawares.

{ *Hebrews* 13:2 }

I SET HIM FREE

I saw the angel
in the marble and carved
until I set him free.

⟨ Michelangelo ⟩

Believing in
Angels

RECEIVE WITH AN OPEN HEART

You can't receive the gift of an angel with a closed heart.

If you didn't manifest living with an open heart,

you would close yourself off from those possibilities.

OPEN YOUR HEART!

Believe,

and you will RECEIVE.

" The Wave "

Jane Seymour

WITH FAITH, ALL THINGS ARE POSSIBLE

*I*t is not easy to believe. But the rewards that come with faith are great: peace, confidence, love, security, happiness, healing and an open heart.

Faith makes things possible,
not easy.

{ Author Unknown }

HEAVEN TO YOUR SOUL

A little faith

will bring your soul to HEAVEN,

but a lot of faith

will bring heaven to your SOUL.

{ Author Unknown }

THROUGH THE LOOKING-GLASS

Alice laughed. "There's no use trying," she said.

"One can't believe impossible things."

"I daresay you haven't had much practice,"

said the Queen. "When I was your age,

I always did it for half an hour a day.

Why, sometimes I've believed as many as six

impossible things before breakfast."

{ Lewis Carroll }

ON A WING AND A PRAYER

I love the idea of prayers being taken up to heaven on wings.

Faith furnishes prayer with wings,

without which it cannot soar to

heaven.

{ St. John Climacus }

A FRIEND IN NEED

Nicole's husband had lost his job, and they were about to lose their house. She tried not to worry, but anxiety consumed her. Desperate, she called her best friend JoAnne, who reminded her of Matthew, chapter six, in the Bible. "It says to look at the birds in the sky. They don't sow or reap, but the Lord feeds them. And God loves you so much more than the birds!"

Not an hour later, Nicole stepped out on to her back patio and saw that it was covered with worms. Dozens of birds were feasting on the unexpected lunch. "God really does feed the birds," she thought, hopeful that it was a sign.

The next day, Nicole found an unmarked envelope outside her front door. It was stuffed with cash—enough to pay her mortgage for several months and save her house. As much as they loved her, none of Nicole's friends had that much money to spare. She never discovered the identity of the angels who had blessed her family.

KNOWING YOU HAVE WINGS

Be like the BIRD that,

passing on her FLIGHT awhile

on BOUGHS too slight,

feels them give way beneath her,

and yet SINGS,

knowing that she hath WINGS.

{ *Victor Hugo* }

HEAVEN HERE IN THIS WORLD

One of the hardest lessons
we have to learn in this life...
is to see the divine, the celestial,
the pure in the common,
the near at hand—to see that heaven
lies about us here in this world.

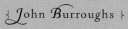

{ John Burroughs }

BE OPEN

Keep your heart and your mind open to the possible

and the impossible.

Miracles
are not contrary to nature,
but only contrary
to what we know about nature.

{ St. Augustine }

LISTEN TO THE MESSAGE

I'm forever grateful that my sister Annie
is such a wise and brave listener:

When my breast biopsy was diagnosed malignant, I was desolate. I sobbed and sobbed—for my children, for myself, for everyone in the world who has no hope. Exhausted and empty, I asked the universe for help. An incredible sense of peace and calm came over me.

The next day, I received three "messages." While waiting in the doctor's office, I saw a magazine headline: "2 out of 3 Healers Have Near Death Experiences." I was training to be a healer. I then read an article about a child whose brain tumor was only correctly diagnosed when his parents asked for a second opinion. We shared the same last name. And that evening, I met a plastic surgeon who told me that much of his work was not cosmetic, but reconstructive—for women misdiagnosed with breast cancer. This was more than coincidence. I called my doctor and asked for a second opinion.

One week later, the surgeon phoned to tell me my previous diagnosis was incorrect. My lump was benign. When I flew upstairs to tell my husband that my life had been spared, I found he was staring at a computer screensaver of the universe.

Annie Gould

On the Wings of Angels

BELIEVE IN MIRACLES

I have many friends who do not believe in luck.

They believe in blessings. Likewise, I do not believe in coincidences.

I believe in miracles.

A coincidence is a small miracle in which God chooses to remain anonymous.

Author Unknown

GOODNESS SHALL FOLLOW ME

The ANGELS…regard our safety,

Undertake our defense, direct our ways.

And exercise a constant SOLICITUDE

That no EVIL befall us.

⊰ John Calvin ⊱

M O T H E R ' S   M E S S A G E S

*J*ust after my mother Mieke passed away, my sisters
noticed that at their feet—where they always sat
and watched her—was a white feather. They looked
around the room and found no source of feathers.
When they called her close friend to tell her the
news, she was in my mother's house, and said she
had just discovered a white feather under the
portrait of my mother that I had painted.

Since then, Mieke's white feather has appeared
in our lives many times in many places.
Sometimes it will show up humorously, like at a
party we're sure she didn't want to miss.

But it most often appears when we are in a moment of indecision, when we don't quite know what to do. James found one in a script he was having trouble working with. I just found one in my girlfriend's car.

My mother lived with an open heart, and we believe she is still very much in our lives. As soon as we see the feather, it instantly puts us into a conversation with her, and we can hear her advice. By constantly reminding us of her presence, she continues to share her wisdom and love with us even though she cannot physically be here.

LOOKING UP

*I*f you want to improve the view, look up!

I believe that if one always
looked at the skies,
one would end up with wings.

{ *Gustave Flaubert* }

Jane Seymour

HOPE HAS WINGS

O welcome, pure-ey'd Faith,
white-handed Hope,
Thou hovering angel,
girt with golden wings!

{ John Milton }

WAITING FOR AN ANGEL

I am on the heart transplant list. When I was thirty-two years old
and pregnant, I was diagnosed with congestive heart failure.
Since then, I have had a defibrillator implanted and am on a heart pump.
I am very independent, and it's hard for me to accept the help I now need.
I have always had an open heart and would rather do for others.

I was thrilled when I saw your open heart necklace with angel wings
because I thought it was so fitting: One heart could represent mine,
and the other is the heart I will get that an angel will bring to me.
Because it will be an angel that will donate their heart.

{ *Lynne*, Joliet, Illinois }

WHISPERS OF LOVE

Angels descending, bring from above,

Echoes of mercy, whispers of love.

{ Fanny J. Crosby }

Familiar Angels

OUR ANGELS, OUR FRIENDS

Angels walk among us.

Angels speak through us.

But what about the angels who are "us"?

THE PEOPLE WE KNOW AND LOVE DEARLY—

Our family and friends—

who inspire us with their love.

STRANGERS WHO GO OUT OF THEIR WAY

to comfort or care for us.

THESE, TOO, ARE *angels.*

MY FATHER'S LOVE

The day before he died, my father and I had a long
conversation about the possibility of heaven. He was a
humanist, and he fervently did not believe in heaven.
Jokingly, I asked him to give me a little haunting
should he be wrong. He chuckled and agreed.
It was the last time I ever saw him.

Not long after he died, my life fell apart. I lost
everything financially and emotionally. I had no idea
how I was going to move ahead. It was then that I
received the call to play "Dr. Quinn." I have
always felt that this unique role, playing a doctor
in a historical period, was a gift from my dad. My
father was a doctor who shared his passion for the

history of medicine with me my entire life.
We visited the Museum of Medical
History. I had a microscope at the age of
seven, watched surgeries at the age of ten and
worked as an auxiliary nurse in his hospital.
It was part of our special bond.

No one knew I had that background, and yet,
in my moment of greatest need, I was given
this special role that enabled me to support
myself, raise my kids and continue in my life.
I'd like to believe it was his "haunting," and that
he was sending me a message of love from heaven.

*An angel is someone
who helps you believe
in miracles again.
And that is a friend,
lover, child.*

{ Author Unknown }

THE STRANGER ON THE WALL

*M*y mother always used to say if you thought life was tough, you should go help someone else. We believe my mother helped my sister do just that after she passed:

The house was abuzz, all of us busy making arrangements for my mother's funeral the next day. I looked outside and noticed a young man whom none of us recognized, sitting on the front wall. I could see at once that he was ill. I helped him inside, told him he was safe and to rest— that I would look after him. He slept peacefully for three hours, and feeling better, he left, promising to see a doctor.

The following day, I found a card on the wall: "Thank you for your kindness to a stranger in his hour of need at such a sad time in your life. You are an angel. Signed, A Friend."

I will never know why he chose my wall to sit on, or why I had so little hesitation in trusting him. I think maybe he was an angel sent by my mother. She knew that comforting another would give comfort to me.

Annie Gould

ANGELS IN DISGUISE

There have been so many people I have found to be angels in disguise.

Two of them came to me in the form of foster parents. I was fourteen

when I was sent to live with them and their two children.

I was abused and felt alone, but they took me in with open arms.

They showed me that it was okay to love and to be loved.

They have always been there for me.

Without them, I wouldn't be the woman that I am today. I hope someday

that I can be an angel for someone else, as they were for me.

{ Deb Small }

THE FIRE OF FRIENDSHIP

The closest people in my life are the ones who can set my soul on fire
when it has gone out. My husband, our children, my sisters,
my friends can rekindle me with something as simple as a smile,
a hug or an encouraging word.

In everyone's life, at some time, our inner fire goes out.

It is then burst into flame by an encounter

with another human being.

We should all be thankful for those people

who rekindle the inner spirit.

{ Albert Schweitzer }

GIVE AS THE ANGELS GIVE

An open heart has infinite love to give.

If instead of a gem, or even a flower,
we should cast the gift of a loving thought
into the heart of a friend—
that would be giving as the angels give.

{ George MacDonald }

SOMEONE YOU'VE KNOWN FOREVER

Isn't it amazing when we make an immediate connection
with someone the very first time we meet them? We feel as if
they have been with us forever. Perhaps they have.

An angel is someone you feel like
you've known forever...
even though you've just met.

{ Author Unknown }

MY ANGEL, MY FRIEND

In one year, my mother died, my grandmother died and my husband

committed suicide. I was left a single mother raising two children with no

support system until my best friend Valerie came to my aid.

She cared for my family in every way, without being asked, and in beautiful

ways that weren't "obvious." I will be eternally grateful to Valerie.

She is not just an angel to me, but to everyone who crosses her path.

} Julie, Palmyra, New York {

FRIENDS LIFT US UP

Friends are angels who lift us to our feet

when our wings have trouble remembering

how to fly.

{ Author Unknown }

Baby Angels

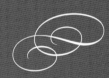

GIVE LOVE FREELY

Images of baby angels are present in art around the world—

and for good reason.

There is something so precious and innocent about children.

THEY GIVE THEIR LOVE FREELY,

without constraint, prejudice or fear.

How open our lives would be

IF WE ALL LOVED *like we did when* WE WERE YOUNG!

WHAT MAKES US STRONGER

Our twin boys Kris and John were born six weeks early via an emergency C-section because I had developed preeclampsia. While they were perfectly beautiful, we lived on pins and needles for the first few months of their lives because they needed round-the-clock observation to make sure they were breathing correctly. Johnny turned blue twice, and we had to rush him back to the hospital. It was a very frightening time—watching our babies live on heart monitors, jumping at every little beep. But like all trials, it didn't last forever. Our family made it through. In fact, it brought us closer together.

The boys are now healthy fourteen year olds. Although they are teenagers, they are still, like our other children, our baby angels.

WHERE DID YOU COME FROM, BABY DEAR?

Where did you come from, baby dear?

Out of the everywhere into here.

Where did you get your eyes so blue?

Out of the sky as I came through...

Whence that three-corner'd smile of bliss?

Three angels gave me at once a kiss...

But how did you come to us, you dear?

God thought of you, and so I am here.

{ George MacDonald }

INNOCENCE ON EARTH

A babe in the house

is a wellspring of pleasure,

a messenger of peace and love,

a resting place for innocence on earth,

a link between angels and men.

Martin Farquhar Tupper

CHILD COMFORTS

Children love to be held. It makes them feel safe, comforted, loved.
But they give those same blessings to the person holding them.
In fact, I think they give a bit more.

When our son Johnny was six years old, we were visiting with his namesake, Johnny Cash. As we all sat in his kitchen, he sang along with his last album for us. By that time in his life, he was quite old, and very sick—not the type of person a young child would usually gravitate to, but that's exactly what little Johnny did. Our son instinctively climbed up onto his lap and, quite unlike his usually boisterous self, sat still and hugged the older singer for forty minutes.

When he finally let go, Big John said to him, "You know what, I wanna thank you, John. You ministered to me." We all asked him what he meant. "I was in great pain," he explained, "and he just healed me. When he was holding on to me, I felt the presence of God."

Our Johnny is now recording his own music at the age of fourteen. Maybe Johnny Cash is his angel.

BAND OF ANGELS

*T*here is a universal language. It is spoken in smiles.

I've heard that little infants converse by smiles and signs

With the guardian band of angels that round them shines,

Unseen by grosser senses; beloved one! Dost thou

Smile so upon thy heavenly friends, and commune with them now?

{ Caroline Anne Southey }

GOD'S NOBLEST WORK

Some say children can see things we adults can't. I'm convinced this is true. After my mom passed away, my three-year-old granddaughter and I talked about her often. I would always ask, "Where is my mommy?" Her answer would always be "up in heaven."

Recently, I was going through a tough time. I took my granddaughter to our favorite restaurant, near the church my mom had attended. When I asked her, "Where is my mommy?" her answer was different. "She's standing right behind you,"

she said, looking over my shoulder and
smiling. I shot around and saw nothing, but
I am convinced that my mother was there.
I know now that she watches over me like
an angel, and will always be right behind me
when times are tough.

{ Sue Buetow, Shakopee, Minnesota }

The Angel Within

FIND THE ANGEL IN YOU

On a number of occasions, I have found myself

doing something or going somewhere

for no specific reason, and then a miracle occurred.

I STRONGLY BELIEVE THAT WITH AN OPEN HEART,

You can receive the guidance of angels

and find the ANGEL WITHIN YOU.

A COMPELLING CRASH

One evening after visiting Warren Beatty, my ex-husband and I were driving on a windy road in Los Angeles far up in the hills. As we made our way home, we passed a crash scene full of ambulances, fire brigade and police. We would normally have turned around and gone in the other direction as the road was blocked, but I was compelled to check it out. To this day, I have no idea why I did this.

I jumped out of the car, ran toward the crash, looked inside and saw a girlfriend of mine covered in blood. She hadn't been able to communicate with the medical workers until she recognized me. She was near death, so I rode in the ambulance with her to the hospital, stayed with her in intensive care and helped locate her family.

She recovered completely, but I often still wonder: Why did I unconsciously find myself going to that scene? Why was I there? What unseen force pulled on my being, bringing me to my friend in her hour of need?

MINISTERING ANGEL

*W*hile this woman's husband is serving his country, she is serving herself, her soul and others:

I am an army wife. The lifestyle is rough. Deployment is difficult. However, each day I wake up with a choice. Do I close my heart off to the world and try to shelter myself from the pain? Or do I keep on living life with an open heart and embrace each new day as a gift from God? I've chosen to keep an open heart. I've chosen to not only survive my husband's deployment but also to thrive through it.

I volunteer for a humanitarian aid ministry because there are so many people experiencing much more difficult circumstances around the world. And I believe that by reaching out to others, we truly will be blessed in return.

{ Noree, Rockford, Illinois }

A DIVINE MISSION

There are those whom we think of as angels whose good works are obvious, Mother Teresa, for example. But there are others whose mission is perhaps not grand, but no less profound. They are sent to remind us of the importance of love.

One of my dearest friends is such an angel. Though she is physically limited, spending most days confined to bed on a respirator, her spirit soars. To be in her presence is to feel the touch of the divine. Her communications are always positive, full of hope or compassion for someone less fortunate. She reminds me that the only thing in life that truly matters is how we treat others.

{ Mary Ann Marino }

To love another person

is to see the face of

God.

{ Victor Hugo }

THE VOICE WITHIN

For, as it is written in the book of the Prophets:

"And the ANGEL that spoke in me, said to me..."

He does not say, "Spoke TO me," but "Spoke IN me."

{ St. Augustine }

The Light From Within

People are like stained-glass windows.

They sparkle and shine when the sun is out,

but when the darkness sets in,

their true beauty is revealed only if

there is light from within.

⟨ Elisabeth Kübler-Ross ⟩

OPEN YOUR HEART

Open your heart and let love in

Open your heart and hear it sing

Love is within you and longs to be free

To heal your pain and let you see

The joy that is giving and feeling love

The power of feeling the strength from above

We are all of one piece and love will win

So open your heart and let love in.

{ Annie Gould }

Art Titles and Descriptions

Page 2: Open Heart Angel XXI
Watercolor with pen and ink on paper
6¼" × 4"

Page 6: Radiant Open Heart Angel II
Watercolor with pen and ink on paper
10" × 8"

Page 10: Open Heart Angel VII
Watercolor with pen and ink on paper
10" × 8"

Page 12: Peace
Oil on canvas
18" × 24"

Page 15: Open Heart Angel
Watercolor and graphite on paper
6¼" × 4½"

Page 16: Together Forever
Oil on canvas
20" × 16"

Page 18: Words of Wisdom Bouquet I
Mixed media on paper
29" × 21¼"

Page 20-21: Designs for Bookmarks—Violets
Watercolor on paper
8" × 2½"

Page 25: Friends by the Bay
Watercolor with pen and ink on paper
4" × 6"

Page 26: Open Heart Angel XXIV
Watercolor with pen and ink on paper
8¾" × 6"

Page 28: Johnny Easter Eggs
Oil on canvas
11" × 15"

Page 31: Open Heart Angel IX
Mixed media on paper
10" × 8"

Page 34-35: Words of Wisdom Bouquet I
Mixed media on paper
29" × 21¼"

Page 37: Remarkable Changes: The Wave I
Watercolor on paper
8" × 10"

Page 38: Boat on a Lake (partial view)
Watercolor on paper
21" × 28½"

Page 42: Open Heart Angel II
Watercolor with graphite on paper
6" × 4"

Page 45: The Wave (with Open Heart)
Watercolor with pen and ink on paper
6" × 8¾"

Page 46: Clouds VI: "Five Poems"
(set designs for the Houston Ballet)
Watercolor on paper
15" × 29½"